What Would THE HOFF *Do?*

WHAT WOULD THE HOFF DO?

An Hachette UK Company
www.hachette.co.uk

Summersdale Publishers Ltd
Part of Octopus Publishing Group Limited
Carmelite House
50 Victoria Embankment
LONDON
EC4Y 0DZ
UK

www.summersdale.com

Printed and bound in Malta

ISBN: 978-1-78685-781-1

Disclaimer: this product is unofficial and is not affiliated with or endorsed by David Hasselhoff.

DAVID HASSELHOFF

What Would

THE HOFF

Do?

MITCHELL ADAMS

summersdale

Life Lessons From
THE HOFF

LESSON NO.1:
BELIEVE IN YOURSELF.

I'm six foot four,
an all-American guy,
and handsome and
talented as well!

My problem is people
seem to laugh at me, but
the one that laughs harder
than anybody is me.

I THINK PEOPLE RESPECT ME BECAUSE THEY FEEL LIKE – I'M KIND OF LIKE CHRISTMAS. YOU CAN'T GET RID OF ME. I JUST KEEP COMING BACK.

Lesson No.2: Age is just a number.

I'VE GOT TWO BAD KNEES
AND A BROKEN BACK,
BUT I'M STILL DANCING.

I feel
like Elvis.
Only alive.

I let
people down
easy with
inspiration.

LESSON NO.3:
MOST PEOPLE SEE
THE BEST IN OTHERS.

I think people
know that I've got
a good heart.

WITHOUT SUSHI
THERE WOULD
BE NO DAVID
HASSELHOFF,
BECAUSE SUSHI
IS LIKE THE
PERFECT WAY OF
DESCRIBING THE
INSIDES OF DAVID
HASSELHOFF. HE
IS LIKE A PROTEIN,
CLEAN AND EASY.
THAT'S HOW I FEEL
ABOUT MYSELF.

_____

I love women
but I don't
understand
them.

LESSON NO.4:
DON'T WAIT FOR SUCCESS
TO COME TO YOU.

The phone didn't ring for a long time, so I stopped waiting for it to ring and started making the calls myself.

I'M PRETTY TOUGH ABOUT PHYSICAL **PAIN.** EVERYTHING ELSE I JUST LAUGH OFF.

I'VE GOT TASTE; IT'S INBRED IN ME.

Life Lessons From
THE HOFF

LESSON NO.5:
ALWAYS BE ABLE TO LAUGH AT YOURSELF.

I think laughter is the best medicine. If you can't laugh at yourself, then you can't laugh at life and the silliness of it all.

Failure usually works for me in the end.

THE PROBLEM WITH ME IS THAT NOTHING EMBARRASSES ME.

Lesson No.6: Don't ask questions.

I DON'T CARE WHY
THEY LOVE ME, AS LONG
AS THEY LOVE ME.

I embrace everything.

If you don't
respect me
you're not
gonna get that
respect back.

LESSON NO.7:
DON'T LET UP ON YOUR EXERCISE GAME.

I once didn't work
out for six weeks.
It took me forever to
get the weight off.

**CELEBRITY
MEANS THAT
I CAN AFFECT
PEOPLE IN
A POSITIVE
WAY.**

———————————————

**Ninety-nine per cent
of people now call
me The Hoff – and
it's out of respect.**

LESSON NO.8:
DON'T LET ANYTHING

If you stand still
long enough,
you'll get stuck.

I AM ANTI-VIAGRA.

I AM THE HOFF.

**WHEN I WAS
YOUNGER I WAS
TERRIFIED OF
GIRLS. I WAS SO
PETRIFIED THAT
I HAD TO WRITE
DOWN CHAT-UP
LINES AND
LEARN THEM.**

Life Lessons From THE HOFF

LESSON NO.9: ALWAYS LOOK OUT FOR NUMBER ONE.

When I was out trying to save the world, I forgot to save myself.

**This is not about
making money – this is
about following my heart,
challenging myself and
having fun.**

I FEEL LIKE I'M 40.
MY DAD'S 87
AND HE'S STILL
GOING.

Lesson No. 10: You've gotta be in it to win it.

IF YOU'RE NOT IN
THE GAME, YOU CAN'T
HIT A HOME RUN.

Come on, I'm a television star. Nobody on television is curing cancer.

Everywhere
I go, it's
The ~~Hoff~~.

LESSON NO.11: DON'T BELIEVE EVERYTHING YOU SEE ON TV.

Image is what people perceive my life to be. It's nothing like the truth.

IT'S THE DREAM OF EVERY PARENT TO BE ABLE TO HELP THEIR CHILDREN SUCCEED.

You feel like you
can't go anywhere.
The analogy is you get
the best table in the
restaurant but everybody
watches you eat.

LESSON NO.12:
DON'T BE AFRAID
OF CHANGE.

And sometimes the hardest thing you can do is walk away. But you got to. And, when you do, it changes your life.

I'VE HAD A GREAT RIDE, AND I'M VERY HONOURED TO HAVE BEEN IN THIS BUSINESS. I'M HAPPY IF I MANAGED TO AFFECT PEOPLE IN A POSITIVE WAY.

IF I HAD TO DO IT
ALL OVER AGAIN
I THINK I WOULD
PREFER JUST TO
BE AN ACTOR,
A SINGER, AND
NOT HAVE THE
FAME TOO MUCH.

Life Lessons From
THE HOFF

LESSON NO.13:
LIFE ISN'T
ALWAYS FAIR.

When you realize that life
isn't fair, you don't act out,
you don't get overly wasted,
you don't get self-indulgent.
You just move forward.

When you're on
stage, you're in control.
No one can get to you.

THE PRESS ISN'T REALLY THAT BAD. MY KIDS SAY, "DAD, FORGET ABOUT IT, IT'S BIRD PAPER. IT DOESN'T MEAN ANYTHING." AND THEY'RE RIGHT. THE TIME TO WORRY IS WHEN THERE'S NO PAPARAZZI.

Lesson No. 14: Don't be afraid to toot your own horn.

GETTING IN SHAPE FOR THIS ROLE, WHICH IS INCREDIBLY DEMANDING, VOCALLY, HAS BEEN A LOT OF HARD WORK, BUT I'M NAILING IT. I'M EVEN KIND OF, AT TIMES, BLOWING MY OWN MIND, BECAUSE I AM EVEN ABLE TO TALK RIGHT NOW.

The hardest line that I ever had to say in my life was "I'm David Hasselhoff."

That's one of the good things about being recognizable — if you need a quick escape, the cabbies will take care of you.

LESSON NO.15:
IT'S NEVER TOO LATE TO DREAM A NEW DREAM.

I have a Guinness Book of World Records entry as the most-watched person on television; now I have a new entry as the only man who has a crab named after him.

THE HOFF HAS BECOME LARGER THAN LIFE, SO I CAN'T DO ANYTHING SMALL ANY MORE.

Before long, I'll have
my own channel –
I'll be like Barney.

LESSON NO.16: NEVER STIFLE YOUR CREATIVITY.

All I want to do is be on stage. A performer needs to perform.

I'M A GUY WHO MAKES MISTAKES.

IN A
CORNBALL
WAY, I THINK
BEING A
CELEBRITY
IS ABOUT
MAKING A
DIFFERENCE,
TOO.

Life Lessons From
THE HOFF

LESSON NO.17:
UTILIZE YOUR
NATURAL TALENTS.

My wife is the dancer,
but I certainly know
how to sing.

In life, you either watch TV or you do TV.

THE TALENT THAT I WAS BLESSED WITH WAS REALLY FOR THE THEATRE.

Lesson No. 18:
There's no such thing as failure.

THAT WAS A LONELY TIME,
BUT I DON'T LOOK AT IT
AS FAILURE, I JUST
LOOK AT IT AS LIFE.
S**T HAPPENS.

I look good, but I probably have the insides of Elvis.

I find it a bit sad that there is no photo of me hanging on the walls in the Berlin Museum at Checkpoint Charlie.

LESSON NO.19:
FIND YOUR TRUE
CALLING.

I can make
people smile. I
watched Elvis do it.
I watch Muhammad
Ali do it. Now
I can do it too.

A LOT OF
AMERICANS
DON'T GET
PANTO. I
FIND IT EASY.
AFTER ALL,
MY WHOLE
LIFE IS A
PANTO.

If I mess up, it becomes big no matter what it is, so if I do something positive, it has to be equally big.

LESSON NO.20:
DON'T LET ANYONE ELSE STEAL YOUR LIMELIGHT.

I found it very difficult to be in the audience. I like to be on stage; I feel safer on stage because I'm in control.

THE HOFF HAS
TAKEN OVER DAVID
HASSELHOFF.
DAVID
HASSELHOFF
REALLY DOESN'T KNOW
WHO HE IS ANY MORE.

I'M A CHEESY OVER-THE-TOP MEGALOMANIAC WITH A DEEP VOICE AND THE MOST AMAZING PECS.

Life Lessons From
THE HOFF

LESSON NO.21:
TURN ADVERSITIES
INTO STRENGTHS.

Even when I make mistakes
and people exploit my
mistakes on television or
on the internet, and they
use it to make fun of me,
it's just kind of working in
my favour at the end.

I'm happy to be me.

IT'S KIND OF PATHETIC BECAUSE HASSELHOFF HAS TURNED INTO THE HOFF AND THE HOFF IS KEEPING HASSELHOFF OUT OF WORK. BUT THE HOFF'S PAYING THE BILLS.

Lesson No. 22:
Keep on hustlin'.

MY ONE AMBITION WAS TO
GO TO BROADWAY, AND I NEVER
GAVE UP ON THAT DREAM.

Susan (Boyle) is responsible for bringing the world together.

Be
gentle with
The Hoff.

LESSON NO.23:
ALWAYS REMEMBER
TO APPRECIATE
YOUR FAMILY.

I have a great relationship with my kids. I'm very proud that we are absolutely, incredibly close. That to me is more important than anything.

IT'S HOW FAST YOU GET UP, NOT HOW HARD YOU FALL.

———————————————

Now who wants to party with The Hoff?

If you're interested in finding out more about our books, find us on Facebook at Summersdale Publishers and follow us on Twitter at @Summersdale.

www.summersdale.com

Image credits

David Hasselhoff illustration on p.3 and throughout by Marianne Thompson; pp.6, 22, 38, 54, 70, 86 © Plasteed/Shutterstock.com; pp.8–9, 24–25, 40–41, 56–57, 72–73, 88–89 © Alexander Baidin/Shutterstock.com; pp.11, 27, 43, 59, 75, 91 © Alex Gorka/Shutterstock.com; pp.12–13, 28–29, 44–45, 60–61, 76–77, 92–93 © Natali Snailcat/Shutterstock.com